Contents

KT-116-328

What is decorated pottery?

Pots, plates, cups, tiles, plaques, figures and vases are different kinds of decorated pottery. Pottery comes in different shapes and sizes. Some is decorated with pictures and some only with colours. Pottery is often beutiful, but it can also be useful. For example, decorated bowls can be used to eat from or store fruit in. Other pottery is ornamental and made just for people to look at and touch, rather than use.

What is decorated pottery made from?

Pottery is made from clay that has been heated in a **kiln** (oven) until it hardens. Clay is a very fine-grained soil found in the ground. When it is moist, it can be moulded and made into different shapes. After you **fire** (bake) the clay in a kiln, it dries out and then keeps its shape. Clay comes in different colours, such as yellow, red, brown and black, depending on where it comes from.

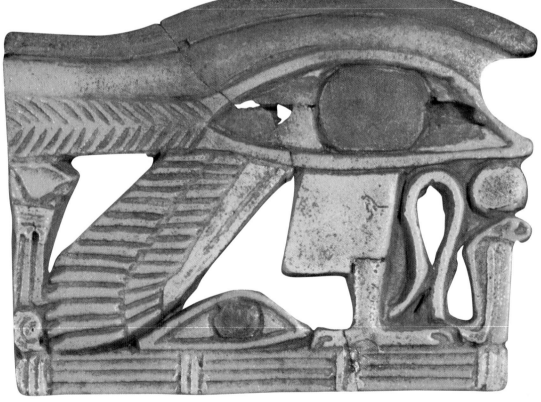

▶ *This pottery amulet, or charm, was made over 3,000 years ago in ancient Egypt. It shows the Eye of Horus and it is supposed to bring good luck to its owner.*

Decorated Pottery

Louise Spilsbury

WAYLAND

First published in 2008 by Wayland

Copyright © Wayland 2008

Wayland
338 Euston Road
London NW1 3BH

Wayland
Level 17/207 Kent Street
Sydney NSW 2000

A catalogue record for this book is available from the British Library.

ISBN 978 0 7502 5406 9

Senior Editor: Claire Shanahan
Designer: Rachel Hamdi/Holly Fulbrook
Project Maker: Anna-Marie d'Cruz
Models: Shannon O' Leary, Ross Zavros, Alex Watson
Photographer: Andy Crawford

Title page, p18/19: Worcestershire willow pattern plate, made by Grainger Lee and
Company, c.1850 (porcelain) by English School, (19th century), Hanley Museum & Art
Gallery, Staffordshire, UK/The Bridgeman Art Library; p6: Wedjat eye amulet (faience)
by Egyptian, Third Intermediate Period (c.1069-664 BC), British Museum, London,
UK/The Bridgeman Art Library; p7: Musicians and dancers at the court of Nasser al-
Din Shah Qajar (1831-96) (ceramic) by Persian School, (19th century), Golestan Palace,
Tehran, Iran/ Giraudon/The Bridgeman Art Library; p8: Photononstop!; p9: © Kevin
Fleming/CORBIS; p10/11, front cover: Odysseus and the Sirens, Athenian red figure
stamnos vase by the Siren Painter, late Archaic, c.490 BC (earthenware) by Greek, (5th
century BC), British Museum, London, UK/The Bridgeman Art Library; p12/13: © The
Trustees of the British Museum; p14/15: Model of a ballgame (pottery) by Mayan,
Worcester Art Museum, Massachusetts, USA/The Bridgeman Art Library; p16/17: Fo
porcelain dog, 17th century, Private Collection/The Bridgeman Art Library; p20/21:
© Succession, Picasso/DACS 2007.

Printed in China

Wayland is a division of Hachette Children's Books,
an Hachette Livre UK company.

Pottery in the past

Remains of pots, dishes and other pottery can tell us a lot about people who lived long ago. Pottery for storing food and water was first made in parts of Japan as long as 13,000 years ago. The first pieces of decorative pottery were probably of gods and goddesses, or jewellery with **symbols** that held special meaning for them. Some pottery was used in religious **rituals** or was painted with pictures that tell stories of everyday life. Looking at pottery can become fascinating when you can 'read' these stories behind the art!

▲ These decorated pottery tiles show musicians and dancers at the court of a shah (king) in Iran.

How to use this book

Background information on each piece of pottery featured, including its designer, date, location and history

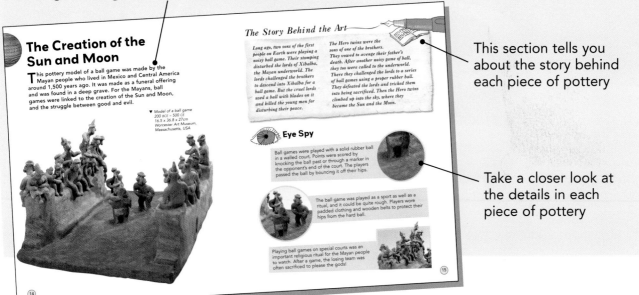

The Creation of the Sun and Moon

This pottery model of a ball game was made by the Mayan people who lived in Mexico and Central America around 1,500 years ago. It was made as a funeral offering and was found in a deep grave. For the Mayans, ball games were linked to the creation of the Sun and Moon, and the struggle between good and evil.

▼ Model of a ball game
200 BCE – 500 CE
16.5 x 36.8 x 27cm
Worcester Art Museum,
Massachusetts, USA

The Story Behind the Art

Long ago, two sons of the first people on Earth were playing a noisy ball game. Their stomping disturbed the lords of Xibalba, the Mayan underworld. The lords challenged the brothers to descend into Xibalba for a ball game. But the cruel lords used a ball with blades on it and killed the young men for disturbing their peace.

The Hero twins were the sons of one of the brothers. They vowed to avenge their father's death. After another noisy game of ball, they too were called to the underworld. There they challenged the lords to a series of ball games using a proper rubber ball. They defeated the lords and tricked them into being sacrificed. Then the Hero twins climbed up into the sky, where they became the Sun and the Moon.

Eye Spy

Ball games were played with a solid rubber ball in a walled court. Points were scored by knocking the ball past or through a marker in the opponent's end of the court. The players passed the ball by bouncing it off their hips.

The ball game was played as a sport as well as a ritual, and it could be quite rough. Players wore padded clothing and wooden belts to protect their hips from the hard ball.

Playing ball games on special courts was an important religious ritual for the Mayan people to watch. After a game, the losing team was often sacrificed to please the gods!

14

15

This section tells you about the story behind each piece of pottery

Take a closer look at the details in each piece of pottery

How is decorated pottery made?

You can make pottery by simply moulding clay into a shape and firing it, or you can use methods such as slab building, **slip casting**, wheel **throwing** and **coiling**.

Slab building

To make flat-sided pots, trays and boxes, you can roll thick slabs of clay and cut them into the right shapes for the sides. Then you join the sides of the pot with slip – a mixture of clay and lots of water. You can make the edges smooth by rubbing them with a wet sponge. The finished box can then by decorated.

Slip casting

In this method, you pour clay slip into moulds made from plaster. Some of the water from the slip soaks into the plaster. The clay sets hard and shrinks in the mould. Then it can be removed from the mould and fired in its new shape. Slip casting is a good way to make identical pots or objects.

◄ *This teapot has been made by pouring slip into a mould. Once the liquid slip sets or hardens, the two sides of the mould are removed, leaving a form in the shape of the mould.*

Wheel throwing

Potters using a wheel throw a round ball of clay onto a circular tray that turns, powered by electricity or a foot pedal. They squeeze and press the clay and pull it up as it turns on the wheel to form a cone shape. Then they push fingers into the middle of the cone to make the dip in the middle of the pot.

◄ *A potter's wheel allows you to make a perfectly round pot, which is almost impossible to do by hand alone.*

What is glazed pottery?

Glazed pottery has a glossy coating that seals and decorates the surfaces. Glazes can be coloured, transparent (see-through), or opaque (not transparent).

Coiling

To make a coil pot, you roll a lump of clay on a table under the palms of your hands until you have a long thin sausage. You attach this to a flat base of clay by coiling it around the edge. By adding more coils in layers, you can form the sides of the pot. The walls are usually smoothed down with tools.

The Song of the Sirens

In ancient Greece, many pots were decorated with stories from Greek myths. These myths are adventure stories involving gods, goddesses, heroes, heroines and **mythical** creatures from powerful animals to monsters. Odysseus, or Ulysses, as he was called by the Romans, was a hero who fought bravely in the famous Trojan War. He had many encounters with mythical creatures on his long journey home by ship. This pot illustrates the story of Odysseus's meeting with the beautiful but deadly Sirens.

◀ *Odysseus and the Sirens 5th century* BCE *British Museum, London, England, UK*

The Story Behind the Art

The Sirens were mythical creatures that had the head of a woman and the body of a bird. They lived on an island and sang beautiful songs that drifted across the sea. The songs bewitched passing sailors who crashed their ships into the rocks around the island and died.

Odysseus had been warned about the Sirens, but he longed to hear their beautiful voices. He told his men to block their ears with beeswax, but asked them only to tie him to the mast. When he heard the Sirens' songs and their promises that they could give him great knowledge and wisdom, Odysseus struggled to escape the ropes to get to them. But the ropes held him tightly, the sailors could not hear his cries, and the ship sailed on to safer seas.

 **Eye Spy**

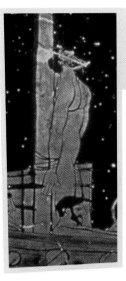

See how Odysseus' body is tense as he struggles to break from his ropes and go to the Sirens.

In ancient Greece, many ships had an eye symbol painted on the front. The Greeks believed that the eye could frighten off evil spirits and protect the sailors and oarsmen on board.

Greek pots like this were made from clay on a potter's wheel. The background and details of the figures and boat were painted in black paint. The red parts of the picture are the unpainted clay colour.

Nasca Nature Spirits

The colourful pottery of the Nasca people is covered with many different animal images, such as this fantastic, mythical bird. The Nasca people lived between 200 BCE and 600 CE along the coast of South America in what is now Peru.

▶ *Double spout and bridge pottery vessel with bird deity 200 BCE – 600 CE British Museum, London, England, UK*

The Story Behind the Art

The Nasca people believed that nature **spirits** controlled their lives, how well their crops grew and how much it rained. The spirits of the air were powerful birds including condors and eagles. Spirits of the land were big cats such as pumas and jaguars. The sea was ruled by killer-whale spirits. The Nasca people did not paint these nature spirits to look like real animals. For example, the fearsome but unusual bird on this pot has the wings and talons of a bird, but the whiskers of a puma or jaguar!

The bird is carrying a human head in its talons. Beheading people was a common type of ritual **sacrifice** in the ancient Andes mountains. The Nasca people often beheaded their enemies. They kept the heads as trophies and made offerings or gifts of them to the nature spirits, in the hope that the spirits would be kind to them.

Eye Spy

The bird wears a mask and a jewelled crown, or headband, to show its importance. Pots like this were often buried in the graves of important people for them to use in the **afterlife**.

The Nasca people usually made pots by coiling. Then they painted on patterns using clay mixed with from black, orange or red. Then they fired and polished the pot.

This bird is sticking its tongue into the head it is carrying. This shows that the Nasca people believed spirits took power from inside trophy heads.

The Creation of the Sun and Moon

This pottery model of a ball game was made by the Mayan people who lived in Mexico and Central America around 1,500 years ago. It was made as a funeral offering and was found in a deep grave. For the Mayans, ball games were linked to the creation of the Sun and Moon, and the struggle between good and evil.

▼ *Model of a ball game*
200 BCE – 500 CE
16.5 x 36.8 x 27cm
Worcester Art Museum,
Massachusetts, USA

The Story Behind the Art

Long ago, two sons of the first people on Earth were playing a noisy ball game. Their stomping disturbed the lords of Xibalba, the Mayan underworld. The lords challenged the brothers to descend into Xibalba for a ball game. But the cruel lords used a ball with blades on it and killed the young men for disturbing their peace.

The Hero twins were the sons of one of the brothers. They vowed to avenge their father's death. After another noisy game of ball, they too were called to the underworld. There they challenged the lords to a series of ball games using a proper rubber ball. They defeated the lords and tricked them into being sacrificed. Then the Hero twins climbed up into the sky, where they became the Sun and the Moon.

Eye Spy

Ball games were played with a solid rubber ball in a walled court. Points were scored by knocking the ball past or through a marker in the opponent's end of the court. The players passed the ball by bouncing it off their hips.

The ball game was played as a sport as well as a ritual, and it could be quite rough. Players wore padded clothing and wooden belts to protect their hips from the hard ball.

Playing ball games on special courts was an important religious ritual for the Mayan people to watch. After a game, the losing team was often sacrificed to please the gods!

The fierce Lion-Dogs of China

This ferocious looking beast is a Chinese lion-dog. Long ago, giant bronze or stone statues of these mythical creatures were created to guard **Buddhist** temples in China. Later, people bought small lion-dogs like this one made of porcelain to protect their homes from evil spirits.

▶ *Fo porcelain dog*
17th century
Private collection

The Story Behind the Art

Around 2,000 years ago, some people in China began to follow the Buddhist religion. The lion was an important symbol for Buddhists, but there were no lions in China, so people did not know what these big cats looked like. In order to make paintings of lions and build statues of lions to guard new Buddhist temples, Chinese sculptors asked Buddhist travellers from India to describe what lions were like.

The animals the Chinese artists created were a mixture of imaginary lions and China's Pekinese dogs! The Chinese word for Buddha is Fo, so these lion-dogs became known as the Dogs of Fo. These ferocious mythical creatures came to symbolise courage, strength and defence of the law and can be seen in China today, standing guard on all kinds of buildings.

Eye Spy

This globe under the lion-dog's paw is a symbol of the way the male lion-dog guards the world. Female lion-dogs are usually shown with a cub under their paw, because they symbolise the importance of family.

Porcelain is a very fine, hard and strong kind of pottery. It is made from white clay that is fired at a very high temperature. Porcelain figures with detailed shapes like this are often made by slip casting.

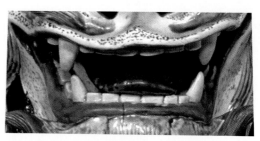

The lion dog has his mouth open to suggest that he is saying the sacred (holy) word 'Om'. Buddhists chant the word 'Om' over and over again as a kind of prayer.

The Willow Blossom Wedding

The story shown on the willow pattern plate is one of a tragic, doomed romance that happened long ago in ancient China. An English porcelain maker designed the pattern around 200 years ago. By linking the design with a romantic story, he cleverly encouraged people to buy his Chinese-style decorated pottery. Different people have changed the willow pattern story over time, but the design of this pottery has remained the same and is still popular today.

◀ *Willow pattern plate*
19th century
Hanley Museum & Art
Gallery, Staffordshire,
England, UK

The Story Behind the Art

Long ago in China, a rich man promised his beautiful daughter Koong-se in marriage to a powerful duke. But Koong-se was in love with her father's poor assistant, Chang. So her father sent the young man away and built a high fence round his garden to keep the lovers apart.

Soon the duke arrived by boat, with a box of jewels as a gift. The wedding was to take place on the day the blossom fell from the willow tree. The night before the wedding, Chang slipped into the palace disguised as a servant. The lovers escaped with the jewels, chased by the father, whip in hand. They eventually escaped by stealing the Duke's ship and sailing to the safety of a secluded island, where they lived happily for years.

But one day the duke discovered where they were. Still hungry for revenge, he sent his soldiers to capture and murder the lovers. The gods were so touched by this doomed romance that they turned the lovers into a pair of doves.

 **Eye Spy**

In Victorian times when this design was created, there was a fashion for collecting objects from China. The willow pattern plate used Chinese-style pagoda houses and decorative patterns.

All of the early willow pattern plates were in blue and white, but the designs were often slightly different. In this one, you can see the boat that the murderous duke arrived in.

In this detail, you can see the wind blowing the blossom of the willow tree, as the lovers escape across the bridge to freedom.

The Origin of Pan Pipes

The artist Pablo Picasso is famous for paintings, drawings and sculpture, but he also made pottery. This pottery plaque shows Pan, a god in Greek mythology. Pan was the god of shepherds, mountains, hunting and music. There are many stories about Pan, but perhaps the most famous is the one about how he created his trademark instrument, the Pan flute or pipe.

▼ *Flute Player and Goat*
Pablo Picasso
1956
Pushkin Museum,
Moscow, Russia

The Story Behind the Art

One day, Pan spotted and tried to catch a beautiful woodland nymph called Syrinx. Nymphs were spirits of the natural world. Pan chased Syrinx from Mount Lycaeum to the banks of River Ladon where he overtook her. In panic, Syrinx shouted for the water nymphs to help her. Just as Pan grabbed her, the water nymphs turned her into the river reeds. When the air blew through the reeds, it produced melancholy sounds. Pan cut some of the reeds and made a flute from them.

The sound Pan made with his pipes was so beautiful that it could enchant all animals, from the wild animals of the wood to those tended by the shepherds, such as sheep and goats.

Eye Spy

The god Pan is shown here as an ordinary man, but in Greek mythology he is a small man with the horns, legs and beard of a goat. In this plaque, Picasso suggests these characteristics by showing Pan playing his flute for a dancing goat.

Picasso used slip-casting to make this plaque. He carved into the mould so the plaque design was in **relief** – raised from the surface. The design was then painted in black to make it stand out even more.

Pan, the goat and the tree are made up of simple, tapering shapes quickly cut into the mould.

Cast a plaque

Have a go at casting a sculpture in the form of a plaque.

You will need:
rolling pin • old, shallow ice-cream tub (empty and clean) • Plaster of Paris powder • clay or plasticine • shaped objects such as shells or small toys • palette knife • poster paints • sequins and beads (optional)

What you do:

1 Roll out a piece of clay or plasticine large enough to fit inside the bottom of a shallow, old ice-cream tub. The thickness will depend on the objects you have chosen to press into it, but aim for 2 – 3cm. Mark a horizontal line about 2cm above the clay on the inside of the tub.

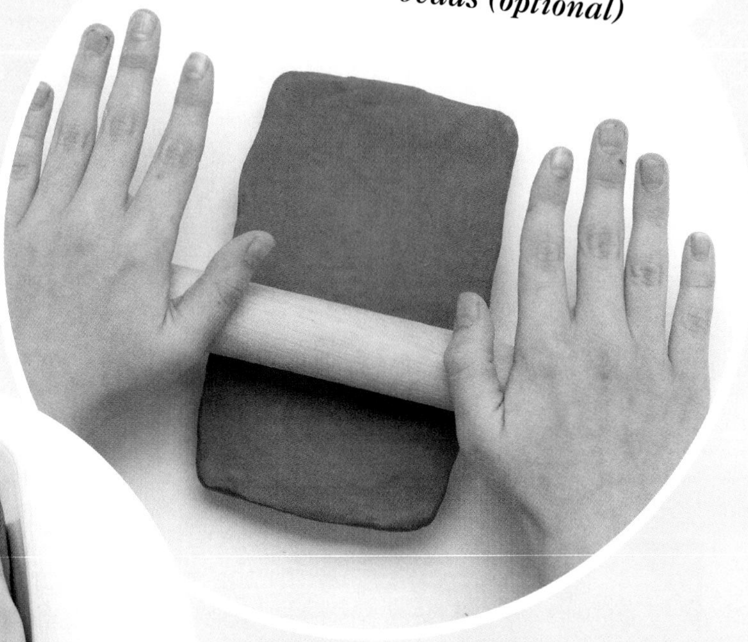

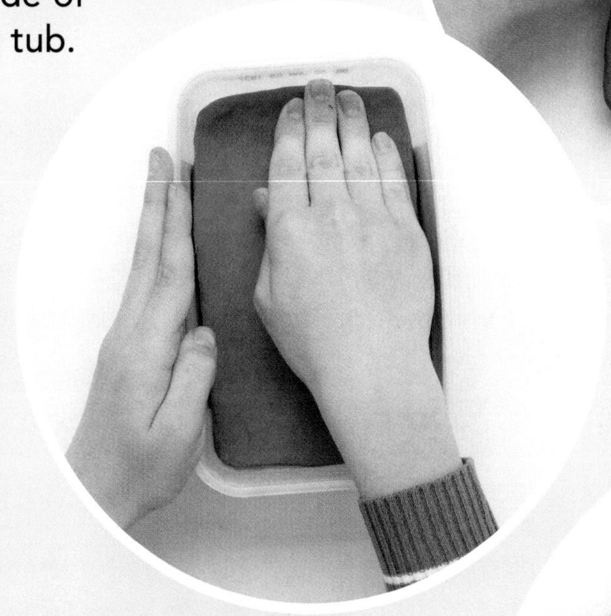

2 Press some shells or other hard objects into the clay or plasticine. Remove them carefully so that neat, clear indentations are left in the plasticine or clay. These are your cast moulds.

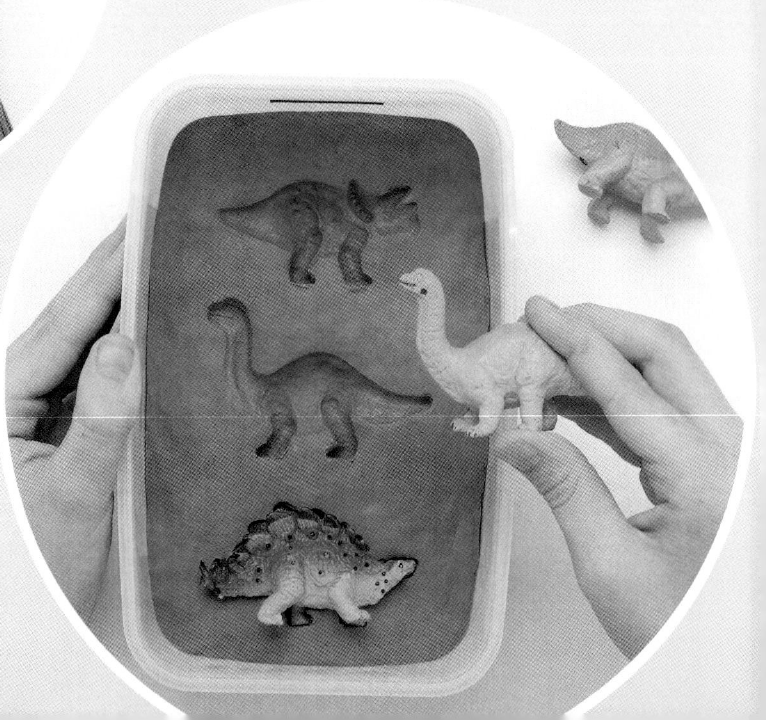

3 Mix the Plaster of Paris with water according to the instructions on the packet and pour it into the tub up to the line. Leave this to set hard.

Top Tip!
Ask an adult to help you mix the Plaster of Paris and pour it in as this can be very messy if you are not careful!

Top Tip!
A few gentle bangs of the tub on a table will help get rid of any air bubbles in the Plaster of Paris mixture once poured into your tub.

4 When you are sure the Plaster of Paris has set, carefully pop out the finished plaque. An easy way to do this is to use a palette knife to loosen the edges, and then turn the tub upside down.

5 Now you can paint and decorate the plaque, and even add sequins or other features to it.

Make a Nasca pot

Make a Nasca pot using the coiling technique.

You will need:
paper • pencil • air dry clay • rolling pin • cup or jar lid • blunt knife • paints in orange, back, yellow and red • paintbrushes

What you do:

1 Think of an animal that has special significance for you. Perhaps it could be a favourite pet or an animal that you like? Now draw the animal using simple geometric shapes such as circles, triangles and squares. Your animal should look **abstract** and simple, like a Nasca animal. You could even add some unusual features like wings to a cat or whiskers to a goldfish!

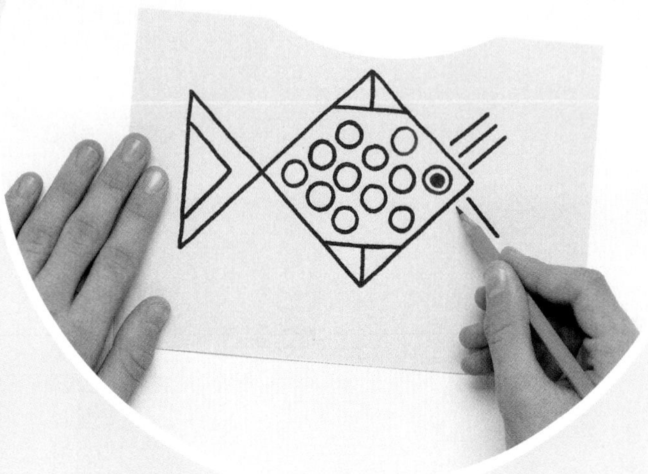

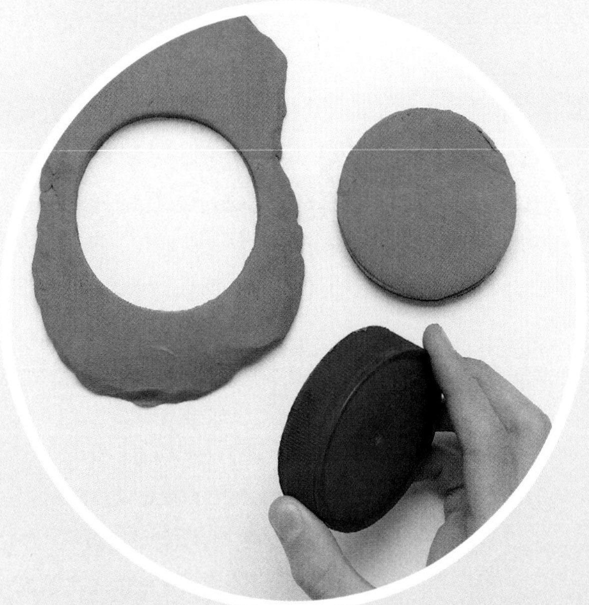

2 Roll a flat piece of clay about 1cm thick. With a cup or jar lid, mark a neat circle and remove it from the piece of clay.

3 Now make your coils. Roll out several long sausages of air dry clay. Make sure they are roughly the same thickness.

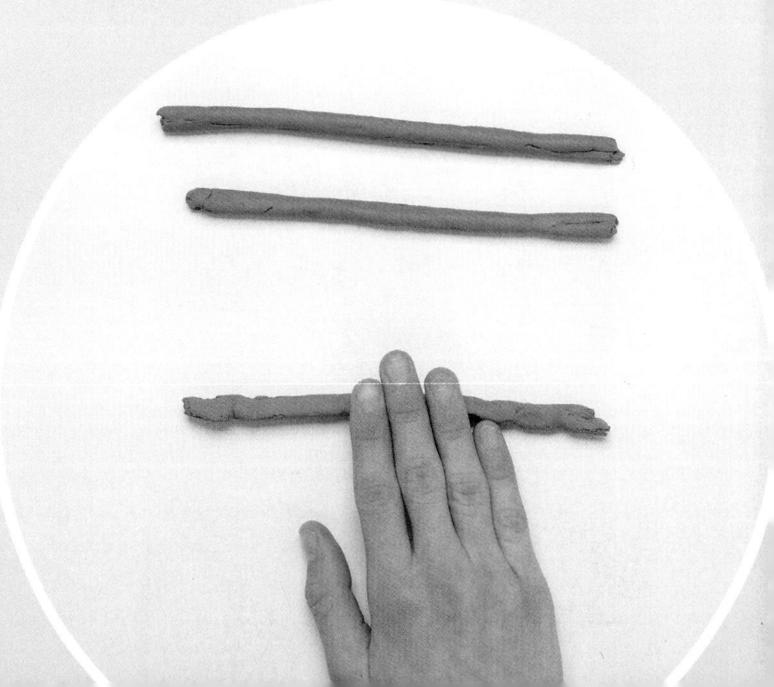

4 Build up the sides by winding the coils one at a time around the base of the pot.

5 When it is high enough, smooth the sides with a blunt knife. You can dampen the knife to help do this. Then leave the pot to dry.

6 When the pot is dry, copy your animal design onto it and colour it in with Nasca colours such as orange, black, yellow and red.

Produce your own plate

Make and paint your own plate.

What you do:

1 Plan a design on the paper plate. Design a pattern for the border (around the edge), and an image for the centre. (If you look at the willow pattern plate on page 18, you see how this plate has a border too.) Perhaps your plate could tell a story, either one that you have made up or one that you like.

Top Tip!
Ask an adult to help you trim the clay to make your plate neat.

You will need:
cling film
• pencils and coloured pencils
• rolling pin • an old plate • air dry clay
• paints • varnish

2 Roll out a sheet of clay about 1cm thick. Lay some cling film over the old plate and then place the clay on top. Ask an adult to trim the edges of the clay to make it neat.

3 When the clay is dry, remove the cling film and the old plate. Now paint your plate with a solid background colour, such as white.

Relief patterns

When your plate is half dry, you could add some small pieces of clay to create a relief design. Just wet the back of your extra clay pieces so that they stick to the plate.

4 When your background colour is dry, you can add your design. Transfer the design by sketching it on in pencil before painting it in. This way you can correct any errors.

5 When the paint is dry, you can varnish the plate so that it looks like it has a glaze on it. You can buy special hooks that stick to the back of plates so you can hang your plate on the wall, or a plate holder to display it on a flat surface.

Glossary

abstract describes art that looks unlike anything real

afterlife the belief that there is some form of life after a person's body dies, usually in a spirit world

Buddhist to do with the Buddhist religion

casting when pottery is made from wet clay that sets in a mould

coiling when pottery is made by building up lengths of rolled clay in coils

fire in pottery, to fire something is to bake it in an oven to make it hard

kiln hot oven used to bake pottery and melt glass

myth/ical/ology to do with a traditional or legendary story

relief shapes that stand out from the background

ritual action usually performed in a religious service that has symbolic value

sacrifice killing an animal or person to please a god or goddess

slip potter's clay that is thinned and used for coating or decorating ceramics

spirit supernatural being

symbol object, picture, letter, number or colour that is used to represent an idea

throwing the way that clay is made into a pot on a potter's wheel

Find out more

Books to read

Clay Characters for Kids by Maureen Carlson (North South Books, 1997)

Clay Projects for Children by Monika Krumbach (A & C Black, 2007)

Greek Myths for Young Children by Marcia Williams (Candlewick, 1992)

The Great Clay Adventure by Ellen Kong (Davis Publications, 2000)

Websites to visit

To find out more about the history of ceramic design, visit the Victoria and Albert Museum at www.vam.ac.uk, or the British Museum website at www.thebritishmuseum.ac.uk.

At www.historyforkids.org/learn/arts/pottery/index.htm, you can learn about the history of clay pots from about 8,000 years ago to present!

www.thejoyofshards.co.uk/projects/maroc shows you how to make a beautiful mosaic from pieces of broken pottery.

Would you like to see decorated pottery that other children have made? Visit www.ecfs.org/Projects/FieldstonLower27111/ARC/index.html to see some great examples from around the world.

Places to go

Museums have great collections of decorated pottery. Try one of these places and don't forget a sketchpad so you can draw your favourites!

The Ashmoleum Museum in Oxford has decorated Italian pottery, ancient Chinese and Japanese pots and many other objects.

The National Museum of Wales, Cardiff, has a collection of Welsh pottery.

The Gladstone Pottery Museum, Stoke on Trent, has displays about how potters prepared, made and decorated pottery in the past two centuries.

Index

Photos or pictures are shown below in bold, **like this**.